DEVOUR

CONSUMING the WORD OF GOD

simply for students

BY JAYSON FRENCH & MARK MOORE

Devour
Consuming the Word of God

group.com
simplyyouthministry.com

Credits
Authors: Jayson French and Mark Moore
Executive Developer: Nadim Najm
Chief Creative Officer: Joani Schultz
Copy Editor: Rob Cunningham
Cover Art and Production: Amy Hood and Veronica Preston
Production Manager: DeAnne Lear

ISBN 978-0-7644-8197-0

10 9 8 7 6 5 4 3 2   20 19 18 17 16 15 14 13 12

Printed in the United States of America.

Dedication

This book is dedicated to my wife Janice (she's led a high school group of girls for years), my son Justin (the high school student living in my house), my son Levi (who wants my job at Christ In Youth), and my second-grade daughter Sydney (who thinks she co-leads a high school group with Mom).

– Jayson

Contents

Introduction

A word for teenagers: This book is for you. We've had countless conversations with students about their frustrations with Bible study. We want to help. You've probably been guilt-tripped by enough people for not studying the Bible regularly. Perhaps you've just never been shown how to start. This book will give tangible solutions. I (Jayson) know you can do this because I watch my son with calculus and physics homework and I'm amazed. When it comes to Bible study, the problem isn't your intellect. Many times, we—your parents and your student ministers—forget that we should be teaching you how to study the Bible on your own.

A word for student ministers: As youth pastors, we've always had a passion for teaching the Bible. However, we've come to realize that teaching students the Bible isn't enough; we need to train students how to devour the Bible on their own. There's danger when they grow amazed at how well we teach; privately, we wonder if they think our words are more powerful than the Bible. We wrote this book so that you could have a resource to empower students to study the Bible themselves.

A word for parents: When did we get old enough to have teenagers? Our kids can't be that old! We can't be that old! Here's the honest truth. The primary responsibility to teach our kids the Word of God doesn't lie with the church; that responsibility belongs to us, as parents. We can be tempted to delegate it to a youth minister, similar to how a math teacher at school is responsible for teaching our children about math. However, that isn't the case. This book is intended to help you train up your child with the Word of God.

So that's the purpose of this book: **Teach students how to devour the Word of God.** We're not talking about a light snack on Sunday mornings or a meal on Wednesday night. We're talking about cooking up your own meal every day. We're all for the occasional devotional book, but it can be kind of like fast food—not enough nutrition to keep you healthy. Teenagers are capable of devouring, digesting, and proclaiming biblical texts.

I (Jayson) have teamed up with a friend and expert in Bible interpretation, Dr. Mark Moore. Together we want to lay out some rich principles in common language so the average teenager can build skills for Bible interpretation.

CHAPTER 1

DEVOUR

What's the craziest thing you've ever eaten? We're not just talking about grandma's oyster-flavored stuffing or peanut butter and mayonnaise sandwiches. We're talking about stuff that's just out there. Unusual food. Peculiar food. Crazy food. Granted, our upbringing and our culture set a standard for our taste buds. What is one person's feast will make another one hurl.

I (Jayson) hate goat cheese. I don't mean that I just don't like it. I hate it, with a white-hot passion. It all goes back to a short-term mission trip I took to the Dominican Republic when I was in high school. We were sitting in a small house, and the host served us some goat cheese. The host was a poor farmer, and he looked on with joy as he provided us with such a "special" treat. The room was hot and humid; the chunk of cheese was the size of my fist, as musty and sweaty as a NFL lineman. I ate mine. It took all my strength to choke it down. Then I looked over at a girl in our group, and she had tears welling up in her eyes because she couldn't eat it but didn't want to hurt our host's feelings. All I could think was "stinks to be you...and good luck with that cheese, because it is awful!"

As our host spoke with students on the other side of the room, our group leader made a fast move. He took that girl's slice of sweaty cheese and handed it to me, giving me that look of "you need to eat this—now." I thought I was going to cry. I looked at the girl, and she just quietly said, "Thank you." You'd think I would have felt chivalrous, but no, I wanted to throw up on her. I gagged with every single bite. I finished, went for a walk, and puked all over my shoes. The smell of cheeses—like Parmesan, blue cheese, or feta, or anything that smells like sweaty socks—makes me gag to this day.

Some things make me gag, but other things make me drool. For example, Thanksgiving at my mom's house is something to be savored: turkey, stuffing, dressing, pecan pie, pumpkin pie, homemade mashed potatoes and gravy, and on it goes. I devour it like a wolverine.

So what is Scripture to you? Sweaty cheese or a Thanksgiving feast? Something you avoid or something you desire? You may never have thought of the Bible as a meal, but the prophets did. Consider the examples of Jeremiah, Ezekiel, and the Apostle John:

"When I discovered your words, I devoured them" *(Jeremiah 15:16).*

The voice said to me, "Son of man, eat what I am giving you—eat this scroll! Then go and give its message to the people of Israel." So I opened my mouth, and he fed me the scroll. "Fill your stomach with this," he said. And when I ate it, it tasted as sweet as honey in my mouth (Ezekiel 3:1-3).

So I [the Apostle John] went to the angel and told him to give me the small scroll. "Yes, take it and eat it," he said. "It will be sweet as honey in your mouth, but it will turn sour in your stomach!" So I took the small scroll from the hand of the angel, and I ate it! It was sweet in my mouth, but when I swallowed it, it turned sour in my stomach (Revelation 10:9-10).

Imagine eating a scroll. It has to feel a little weird on the tongue! However, something happens to people who devour the Word of God. The lives of these three men were radically changed.

The same can be true for you. If you feast on the Word of God, you will change from the inside out. We can't just look at the Word of God like we'd look at a restaurant menu without ever actually placing an order. At some point, you need to get the meal, slice it up, roll it around in your mouth, and consume it. When you devour the Word of God, it becomes a part of who you are. You truly are what you eat. Are you ready to devour the Bible?

The following chapters are going to teach you how to do that. Mark and I collectively have more than four decades of hands-on student ministry experience. We know that most students struggle with studying the Bible. The teenagers we've worked with had heard about the importance of studying the Bible, but they just didn't know where or how to start.

It's crazy that students can pick up an iPad® or a laptop and can figure it out in nanoseconds. But when teenagers open a Bible, most don't know where to begin. Most churches—and more importantly, most parents—haven't done a very good job at teaching students how to read the Bible, let alone study it. So we open our Bibles and play a Russian roulette-inspired style of study by randomly picking a verse, reading it, and then closing the Bible without a clue what we just read. There has to be a better way.

We want to teach you how to study the Bible. We don't want to hand you just another "devo" book to work through. You've probably started a dozen of those in your lifetime, and you still don't feel like you know how to study the Bible. So let's start over. Let's learn how to cook up a "scroll," slice it up, and devour it. After all, *"people do not live by bread alone; rather, we live by every word that comes from the mouth of the Lord" (Deuteronomy 8:3).*

CHAPTER 2

THE AIM IN BIBLE STUDY

Have you ever sat in a Bible study and heard this question: "What does this text mean to you?" It's as if sharing our combined opinions will somehow prompt God's Spirit to show up. In the end, our personal opinion about the meaning of Scripture is almost completely irrelevant. Can you imagine a physics student reading Einstein's equation of $E=MC^2$ and coming up with a personal interpretation? On the test, if she writes, "$E=MC^2$ means that Everyone Matters to Christ Exponentially," she will fail the exam even though her answer is theologically sound.

*What matters is what the **author** was trying to say.* Or put another way: The AIM of Bible study is the Author's Intended Meaning. Every day our lives depend on understanding what other people are trying to communicate. You have to understand traffic signs to drive. If you want to start on the team, you'd better follow the coach's game plan. When you get a text message from a friend, it makes sense because you know the friend and you know the intended meaning. Imagine handing your parents your phone and having them think every text message was written directly to them. That probably would result in some confusion! But when your parents look at the message from the author's point of view, the meaning quickly clears up.

So why would people think they have the right to make the Bible mean whatever they want? It isn't our culture or context that determines biblical meaning; it is what the author intended to say. Everyone may have an opinion, but the opinion that matters most is that of the author.

Getting the AIM can be helped by using your imagination. After reading a passage in the Bible, picture the author (such as Paul or Matthew or Jeremiah) sitting in front of you. Imagine saying to that person, "This is what you intended this passage to mean." And then you present to the author the interpretation of what you just read. If the author looks back at you and says, "Huh?" you know you're wrong. If, however, the author says, "Yep, that's what I meant," then your interpretation is good to go. Obviously this is an oversimplification, but it works 90 percent of the time as an effective filter to weed out most of the silliness that usually follows the phrase, "To me, this passage means...."

Is There Really Only One AIM?

Most of the conversations you have every day have only one meaning. People talk to you, send you text messages, and call you, and you pretty much know exactly what they mean. If you are going to start trying to change the meaning of their words, then you'd better have a good reason for doing so.

Can there be more than one meaning in a Bible passage? Sometimes passages have a double meaning. For example, parables have both an "earthly" meaning and a "heavenly" message. So yes, sometimes the author deliberately designs a double meaning.

However, most of the time, when you are reading the Bible, the meaning is singular, interpretations can be multiple, and applications can be infinite. That may have sounded a little confusing. Let's make it easier to understand. It's like when your mom walks into your bedroom and tells you to get off your phone and "pick up the house." As the author of the command, she had a very specific "meaning" when she gave the order. Now you have to interpret what she meant. So you wonder, was it your room, laundry, dishes, or sweeping?

Application of what you heard could be infinite. You could start with the living room, kitchen, or attic; she just said to pick up the house. Or you could rent a crane and very literally "pick up the house." Sure, that is a possible interpretation, but we all know that it was never her "meaning."

Like your mother, when an author speaks or writes, he or she means something specific. Your first job is to figure out the **meaning**. The author intends to communicate a particular message to a specific audience. Again, the meaning is singular, interpretations can be multiple, and applications can be infinite.

Unfortunately, writers—like mothers—are not always clear. So we have to dig in and study the passage. Sometimes that study shows several possible **interpretations**, and we have to make our best educated guess as to which one the author really meant. In the example of cleaning the house, you have to make an educated guess that your mom specifically wanted the living room and kitchen picked up. Maybe she would love to have the closets and the attic cleaned, too, but that wasn't really what she meant. Make sure you know what is actually God's instruction and what is just your own opinion.

We then attempt to apply the ancient text to a modern situation. There could be dozens of appropriate applications. How you apply and live out this text could be very different from how your parents, classmates, or someone living on the other side of the world might apply it.

Sometimes we just can't seem to understand a biblical text. It seems so vague and mysterious. Keep in mind that *sometimes ambiguity is considered good communication*. Just because a text is confusing does not mean that it is poorly written. Maybe it was intended to be a little vague. For example, sometimes the best movies are the ones that leave us thinking and continuing to ask questions. You love it yet hate it when a great film leaves you thinking about the plot. You leave the theater with your friends and you just know that there will be a sequel because the filmmakers intentionally left you hanging. It's the mark of a great book, movie, or story to let you investigate and wonder.

Ambiguity is a tool that good educators, writers, and filmmakers use. Before you decide "Jesus doesn't make any sense in this story," stop and consider that he may just want you to walk away and think. Jesus' parables were deliberately designed to make people think long and hard about the meaning of the "simple" story. Ambiguity may make a text look confusing, but sometimes the goal is not clear meaning but deep reflection.

So here's a quick summary: There is only one AIM in most passages. Authors speak and write so that their meaning will be clearly understood.

Can We Even Get the AIM?

It is one thing to say there is a single meaning for most Bible passages. It is quite another thing to claim we can get at that AIM. After all, there are two big obstacles in the way: historical distance and pre-understanding. Let's deal with both.

Historical Distance
It doesn't take a rocket scientist to realize that the Bible was written a long time ago. A lot of history and great distance stand between you and the Bible—distance in time, language, culture, geography, and religion. Unless you are 2,000 years old, speak Hebrew or Greek, live

in the Middle East, and eat goats, the Bible is going to be a bit like foreign territory to you. Even though the challenges are real, we have some great tools at our disposal. For example, even though you don't speak Hebrew or Greek, you have really good Bibles in English that you *can* read. And even though the people in the Bible lived a really long time ago, God hardwired your heart to be able to feel compassion for others, even if you've never met them.

Living in the 21st century helps us in our quest to understand and devour God's Word. Go online and you will find a ton of tools that can help bridge this gap of more than 2,000 years. My 12-year-old son can tell you a ton about penguins and India, yet he's never stepped foot in Antarctica or taken a single flight to New Delhi. In many ways, it's never been easier to bridge these gaps.

If the History Channel can take you back in time, can Bible tools do the same thing? Yes! **Translations** help bridge the gap of language[1], a good **Bible atlas** bridges geography, **encyclopedias** bridge culture, and so on. *In short, there is no excuse for not crossing the bridge between the modern and ancient worlds.* We have all the tools necessary to understand (not perfectly but thoroughly) the cultural, historical, geographical, literary, and linguistic world of the Bible.

Just as a musician can train her ears and a student can train his mind, Christians can also train their spiritual perception. How? It comes through obedience. Jesus said, *"Anyone who wants to do the will of God will know whether my teaching is from God or is merely my own" (John 7:17).* The Bible is more like auto mechanics than philosophy. In order to understand philosophy, you need to wrap your mind around deep thoughts. In order to understand auto mechanics, you need to wrap your hand around a wrench. That's certainly not to say that Christianity has no deep thoughts. Theology is obviously a mind-blowing endeavor. Yet it is most often in the *practice* of Christian principles and truths that a person's perception is expanded and certain Bible passages come alive.

Pre-Understanding
A second roadblock that keeps us from getting the AIM is our pre-understanding. What is "pre-understanding"? It is basically our perception about life. My second-grade daughter, Sydney, explained it really well. She says "text to self" relates what she is reading to something in her

own life. "Text to text" relates the book she is reading to a book that she has read in the past. She's also been taught to use "text to world" to relate something from a book to something she has heard about in the world or maybe seen on TV. While these ideas are great for her favorite book, *Splat the Cat* by Rob Scotton, they can offer some challenges when it comes to the Bible.

You have to be careful not to take your life and your experiences and try to make them fit the Bible. People do something similar to us every day. We start telling a story, get halfway through, and they interrupt and say: "I totally understand; one time I did the exact same thing." We sit back, listen to them talk on and on, and think, "No, you didn't even try to understand, and my situation wasn't anything like yours." It can get really annoying when other people try to fit their lives and experiences to match yours. Instead of understanding you, they get ahead of you. Instead of listening to you and trying to understand, they just jump to their own life experiences and make a loose connection to their own past.

A lot of times, unintentionally, we do the same thing with biblical authors. We make it about us, not about the text. Imagine hearing the author of 1 Samuel tell you the story of David's battle with Goliath. You interrupt to say: "I totally understand. This one time I was playing basketball against this really tall guy and...." That's when the author sits back and just listens to you drone on and on with your pre-understanding. He realizes you've missed the point.

Sometimes we don't even realize that we are bringing the baggage of preconceived ideas to a biblical text. It just surrounds us so much that we don't even realize it. Our gender, education, technology, hometown, siblings, and a thousand other things shape who we are, how we think, and consequently what we see in the Bible.

Does a fish know it is wet? That's the problem with our pre-understandings. They surround us and permeate us so they are difficult to identify. Just because you understand something one way in your culture doesn't mean it works in every culture. You can't expect your understanding in a world of iPads and Kindles® to be the same understanding people had 2,000 years ago when they were listening to Jesus and then when the authors were writing the books of the New Testament.

One of the tools we have to help us get beyond our pre-understanding is our *shared emotional experiences*. Part of belonging to humanity means that throughout history, we all experience pain, joy, frustration, love, and other similar emotions and events. We can sympathize with others and break through our previous pre-understandings to a new level of awareness. Additionally, a crisis sometimes thrusts us into a new reality. The death of a friend, a parent's divorce, or a teen pregnancy will instantly change the way we perceive reality, including our reading of the Bible. Suddenly you find yourself reading the Bible with new intensity and interest in order to deal with what life is throwing at you.

Most of those major life issues are bigger than where you live or even when you were born. It doesn't matter if it is the Midwest, England, or India; losing a mom or a dad will always bring pain. That was true 2,000 years ago and is true today. There are some things that, due to our shared emotional experiences, we all understand.

Not only can we share life experiences and universal emotions, we also share *spiritual longings* to know God, to understand the afterlife, to deal with guilt, and to belong. When the Bible describes heaven or hell, when

Jesus teaches on prayer, or when Paul talks about the work of the Holy Spirit, these words tap into universal spiritual longings that resonate with us. We all have a shared sense of eternity in our hearts.

You are not the same person you were three years ago, and obviously in another decade you will be a very different person. Our pre-understandings change, providing us with ever-changing and often increasing insights into the biblical text. Let's explore some principles and guidelines that will help you as you begin to read and interpret Scripture.

Practices of Noble Interpretation

Just as in kindergarten your teacher called on you to practice "fair play" that you already instinctively knew was right, so now, we are calling you to "fair play" when reading in order to effectively understand the Bible. These seven virtues must guide your study of the Bible:

1. **Listen courteously.** Listen to the author as your dialogue partner from his perspective without trying

to force him to say what you *think* he should be saying. If you were to repeat back to him what he just said in your own words, he should nod and say, "Yep, you got it!"

2.   **Listen attentively.** Real listening is hard work. Pay attention to the details, the context, the purpose of what the author is saying, the emotional tone, and what the author is trying to accomplish through the communication.

3.   **Listen generously.** If you love the person you are listening to, you will hear his heart, not just his words, and you will tend to give him the benefit of the doubt when something is unclear or seemingly inaccurate. Do that with the Bible.

4.   **Listen humbly.** We listen to mentors we respect differently than we listen to our little brother, because we assume our mentors have something valuable to teach us. If you take that posture of humility with everyone you listen to (especially biblical authors), you will learn much.

5. **Listen practically.** Listen as if you were reading a recipe from a cookbook or a manual for your new computer. You are going to implement this stuff, so look for practical applications.

6. **Listen artistically.** Every communicative act comes packaged in some genre and form. Pay attention to the artistic presentation, not merely the content of the communication. Read the Bible more like a story than an algebraic formula.

7. **Listen communally.** The Bible was written to the community of God's people, not to individuals. So even if you are studying alone, you should always hear the voices of notable teachers both past and present, whether it is through books, MP3s, CDs, websites, or podcasts.

Conclusion

Our goal in Bible study is the AIM. Yes, there is just one AIM, and yes, we have the tools to comprehend it. Perfectly? No. The point, however, is not perfection but proximity. We are attempting to come close enough to the author that we can listen respectfully. No doubt, there are some obstacles, but these obstacles of historical distance and pre-understanding can be overcome if we want passionately enough to hear what the Bible is saying and if we are willing to make the effort to listen attentively.

Going Further

- Choose a passage of 6 to 10 verses long or one full paragraph (for example, Romans 12:1-8; Colossians 1:15-23; Philippians 2:1-11; or James 2:1-12). Your parents or youth pastor might help you pick a great passage. This will be your text for practicing the principles in the rest of this book.

- Print your text triple-spaced on a piece of paper so you can make lots of notes between the lines. Next, write out about 25-30 observations and 25-30 questions about your text. Go crazy here! No question or observation is too trivial or silly. Here are the kinds of things to look for: patterns, repetition, lists, cause/

effect, conclusions, contradictions, conjunctions, key words, prepositions, pronouns, questions. Who wrote this? To whom? Why? How does this section connect with what came before it and with what follows? If this section of Scripture were not here, what would be missing in the text?

CHAPTER 3

CONTEXT IS KING

If you are to be a legit Bible student, you must learn this mantra: "Context is king, context is king, context is king." There is probably nothing more important for understanding the Scriptures than context. *The most common error in Bible interpretation is using passages out of context!*

Simply put: The context of your passage is the text that immediately surrounds it. Biblical authors didn't just dump a trunk of junk onto the page so you could arrange it how you see fit. Each verse is part of a bigger point (paragraph). And each point is part of a larger discussion (chapter). And these discussions are strung together to develop an overarching story (book). The goal for the Bible student is to see how these various parts fit together.

It is like the parts of a car. Parts connect together so that *the whole is greater than the sum of its parts*. Each part makes little sense without the whole. Or perhaps you could think of it as a river that comes from upstream and flows down to the next little village. Except for the first verse, there is always an upstream. You'd better know what they were doing upstream before you drink the water! And except for the last verse, there is always a downstream; what happens on the banks where you stand will affect what happens below. We must always trace the flow of a thought through the entire book to fully appreciate what is happening in any given spot. To that end, *the goal of this chapter is to learn how to identify the context of any given verse of the Bible and to interpret that verse in the flow of the larger story.*

Warning!

Watch out for two things in particular. First, *memorizing individual Bible verses* has been one of the worst practices for correct understanding of the Bible. Yep, we said it; single Bible verse memorization can be dangerous. Don't get us wrong; Bible memorization is a wonderful thing. In fact, it is probably the single most important exercise for correct understanding of the Bible. The problem comes when we isolate a single verse and commit it to memory but have no idea where it comes from, why it was said, or how it functions in the overall story.

Philippians 4:13 is probably the most misquoted verse of the entire Bible: *I can do everything through Christ, who gives me strength.* This verse is used to transform the average Christian into a superhero. I (Mark) was working out at a gym during a youth conference. A couple of freshmen came in and tried their hand at the bench press. They lay down on the bench and put two 45-pound weights on the bar, totaling 135 pounds, including the weight of the bar. The dull thud on the boy's sternum was a sign that perhaps he had attempted too much.

As our little wannabe bodybuilder groaned and wheezed the bar back up, his friend exhorted him, "You can do it! You can do it!" Then he said it, and I couldn't believe my ears: "You can do all things, all things, ALL THINGS through Christ who gives you strength!" In his defense, the guy did get the bar up (once). But if Christ strengthens us, then why not load up a couple of hundred pounds more?

Open your Bible right now to Philippians 4. Read from verse 10 through verse 20. Now answer these two questions: (1) What topic is Paul really talking about? (2) Was verse 13 a promise or a personal claim of Paul?

Now raise your right hand and promise never to misuse that verse again!

A second bad practice for context is *using Bible quotes as bracelets and bumper stickers*. We have "power verses" affixed to our mirrors or bumpers; they are plastered on our church signs and T-shirts. We thus have power to "Mount up with eagle's wings," "Walk through the valley of the shadow of death," or "Leap tall buildings in a single bound." We seem to feel that the very citation of a passage will ward off demons, sicknesses, annoying siblings, and other icky things. This, in fact, is a very old practice.

The Jews used to wear phylacteries. They were little boxes strapped to the forehead and the left arm, and they contained miniature scrolls of Scriptures (usually Deuteronomy 6:4-6). Why? Because this passage instructs parents to teach the Scriptures to their children, and in verse 8 we read, *"Tie them to your hands and wear them on your forehead as reminders."* The Jewish rabbis took this literally. Then they started competing with each other for the size of their boxes because the bigger the box, the more room for Scripture, and the more room for Scripture, the more obviously spiritual you were (kind of like seeing who has the biggest Bible or the most "Christian" apps on their smartphone). They missed the point. Jesus criticized this very practice in Matthew 23:5.

In order to do proper Bible study you must stop thinking verses and start thinking paragraphs. Only then can you hear what the author intended to say.

Don't you hate to be interrupted? You get halfway through your thought and the other person cuts you off before you can finish. Or maybe you've been in an argument and the other person only hears one phrase or one word and then goes off on you without listening to your entire thought. The first step in hearing a biblical author is to hear his entire thought before you interrupt. But how are you supposed to know?

How to Identify the Context

What we're asking here is simple: How can we know where one thought or paragraph ends and another one begins? Sometimes that's the tough spot when you want to study the Bible. You read one verse, have no idea where or what the author is talking about, and walk away confused. Where do you start? At the beginning of a chapter? Halfway through? So frustrating! Most of the time you just lay the Bible down and go to bed, feeling frustrated because you read but didn't get much out of it.

Well, let's start by agreeing that the paragraphs in the Bible have to be indented somewhere. Who figures that out and how? Well, the *who* is simple—the translators or editors of a Bible version. As a general rule, they get it right. However, you should know that while the texts are inspired, their translations are not. God inspired the text when the authors were writing. What we mean is that God guided the minds of these authors to accurately record his will and words (see 2 Timothy 3:16). People did the work as they tried to take the language from Greek and Hebrew and put it into translations we could understand. The translators did their best, but it is never as good as the original. That includes not only their wording but also their editing.

Sometimes passages in English translations can be misleading. For example, perhaps you have heard that the Bible teaches wives to be in submission to their husbands. That's true. Take a peek at Ephesians 5:22—

For wives, this means submit to your husbands as to the Lord. Unfortunately, some translations include a major paragraph division, including an editor's section title between verses 21 and 22. However, verse 21 says this: *And further, submit to one another out of reverence for Christ.* Our reading of wives submitting to their husbands should be considered in light of the command to submit to one another because of our love for Jesus. In other words, while wives should submit to their husbands, all of us are submitting to authorities in our lives. This illustrates why you need to double-check the section divisions and not merely trust the paragraphs indented in your particular translation. You just need to read a few verses before the passage you are studying and a few verses after. Then ask the simple question: What do these verses have to say about my text?

Don't Read All Bible Books the Same Way

You've probably had a favorite author or some book series you liked to read. You are experienced enough to know that fiction reads differently than nonfiction. Biographies read differently than thrillers. If you want to understand a book of the Bible, it will help if you understand the author and his style. Different authors were inspired to write with different styles. Those styles were meant to capture the attention of different audiences. Some people love to read biographies, while others love to read science fiction. Your biblical text, you see, is like a brick that fits together with other bricks in the overall pattern and structure of a building. Authors "lay their bricks" so as to create a design that catches the eye. The books of the Bible come in a variety of styles. Here is one way to look at them:

Chronological: Genesis, Exodus, Joshua, 1 and 2 Kings, 1 and 2 Chronicles

Biographical: Ruth, 1 and 2 Samuel, Esther, Matthew, Mark, Luke, John

Geographical: Nehemiah, Jonah, Acts

Cyclical: Judges, Job, Ecclesiastes, Song of Songs, Revelation

Logical: Romans, Galatians, Ephesians, Philippians, Colossians, Hebrews

Topical: Leviticus, Numbers, Deuteronomy, Ezra, Lamentations, 1 and 2 Corinthians, 1 and 2 Thessalonians, 1 and 2 Timothy, Titus, Philemon, 1 and 2 Peter, 1–3 John, Jude

Visionary: Isaiah, Jeremiah, Ezekiel, Daniel, Hosea, Joel, Amos, Obadiah, Micah, Nahum, Habakkuk, Zephaniah, Haggai, Zechariah, Malachi

Some books would make very clever screenplays or even theater productions. Jonah, for example, would be a great action movie with some pretty cool special effects. Job, on the other hand, would be a wonderful piece for a reader's theater. And Song of Songs could be a stage play, though minors would need to be stopped at the door! Joshua and Judges would be rated-R action flicks. Each writer uses his own unique style. By identifying them, you will better be able to play mental follow-the-leader with our authors.

Check this out as an example of how an author uses an acrostic as his writing style: Turn in your Bible to Psalm 119. It is the longest chapter in the Bible, with a total of 176 verses. If you will look closely, you will notice that each paragraph is divided into eight verses. (Go ahead

and count a few of them; you know you want to check.)
Pretty cool, huh? Every section begins with a letter of
the Hebrew alphabet starting with *aleph* (the first letter)
and going through *taw* (the last letter). It's the A-Z of
the Hebrew alphabet. In fact, if you want to learn the
Hebrew alphabet, the letters are printed in many English
translations of the Bible, one letter above each section of
Psalm 119. Truly, this psalm is way cooler in Hebrew than
it could ever be in English. This same acrostic pattern is
found in Proverbs 31:10-31 and Lamentations 2.

Determining the Purpose of the Book

There is one last step for fully grasping your context:
Determine the book's purpose. The exact same words
can have very different meanings based on the author's
purpose. Here are four ways you can determine a Bible
book's purpose.

1. **The purpose of a book might be clearly stated.** This
    makes it super easy to figure out why the author
    wrote the book. For example, John states his purpose
    near the end of his Gospel: *These are written so*

that you may continue to believe that Jesus is the Messiah, the Son of God, and that by believing in him you will have life by the power of his name (John 20:31).

2. **The flow of thought throughout the book may reveal its purpose.** This is certainly true of Genesis. There is a refrain throughout the book: "These are the generations" or "This is the account" or similar wording, depending on which English translation you're reading (see Genesis 2:4; 5:1; 6:9; 10:1; 11:10, 27; 25:12, 19; 36:1, 9; 37:2). Genesis moves from Adam to Israel, showing God's sovereign plan unfolding in human history.

3. **The occasion for writing the book may suggest its purpose.** For example, Jeremiah was written against the pressing political backdrop of the invasion by Babylon (modern-day Iraq). Mark was likely written in the shadow of Rome when emperors were worshipped as gods; Revelation was written later, likely when Christians were experiencing persecution from Domitian, the Roman emperor. The setting of a book can give some significant clues as to the purpose of the work as a whole.

4. **Sometimes the purpose of a book is implied by its contents.** The book of Hebrews demonstrates that Jesus is "better" than the old Jewish Temple. A brief glimpse of Proverbs shows the value of getting wisdom. Much more could be said, but these examples illustrate how the content of a book will give you a pretty fair idea of its theme(s) and purpose(s).

Conclusion

Context is king! There simply is nothing more important in Bible study (or everyday conversation, for that matter) than context. Be very careful before pulling out one text as a "power verse." To understand what your author is saying, first try to establish the parameters of the paragraph. Then analyze the structure of the book as a whole, as well as any literary devices. Seeing the structure will not only allow you to comprehend the meaning of the author, it also will enable you to appreciate the artistry and beauty of his craft. Finally, you should understand why he wrote the book in the first place. If you can grab these three things—context, structure, and purpose—you will be well on your way to a thorough understanding of the author's intended meaning.

Going Further

- Using the passage you selected from the assignment at the end of Chapter 2, read through the entire book where your passage is found. If you can't crank out the entire book in one setting, then try to read at least a couple of chapters on either side.

- In a paragraph or two, answer the following questions: How does this text fit into the context before and after my paragraph? If this text were not written, what would be missing from the whole book? Is this text the major point of the book?

CHAPTER 4

HOW NOT TO BE AN UGLY TOURIST WHEN READING THE BIBLE

If you go to Asia, don't point with your feet; it is disrespectful. If you get to Chile and someone across the room purses her lips as if to kiss you, don't flatter yourself; it is just a way of pointing. In India, always shake with the *right* hand. The left hand traditionally was reserved for an act of personal hygiene that you might find a bit shocking. In Africa, don't eat everything on your plate; otherwise your host *will* fill it up again.

The list of cultural peculiarities could go on and on. That's why it is always a good idea to pick up a guidebook whenever you are traveling to another country. In addition to telling you the best places to eat, the best means of transportation, and the major sights to see, it will warn you about particular dangers you might face and any cultural mistakes you might need to avoid. This chapter is like one of those travel guides. We are inviting you to take a trip with us to the biblical world. We hope to help you avoid some of the bigger pitfalls you might encounter while on foreign soil.

What to Look for in Cultural Background

When we are investigating the historical or cultural background of a text, we could look for dozens of things (fortunately, they are all pretty interesting). You might think they don't matter much for the understanding of a text, but they do, so let's look at a few examples:

- **Dress:** Does it really matter what people wore? It mattered to a woman in Luke 8:44. She wanted to be healed, so she touched the "edge" of Jesus' cloak in order to be healed. Why? That just seems weird. When you get those little "why" or "how" questions, that means it is time to go to work. This particular word is used of the tassels that were found on the four corners of a Jewish prayer shawl. If Jesus dressed like a faithful Jew, he surely would have worn one. These tassels were knotted in specific ways, and each knot represented a prayer the man would say (similar to Catholic rosary beads). There was a superstition common in Jesus' day that a righteous man's prayers left a kind of invisible, spiritual "pixie dust" on these tassels as he touched them during his daily prayers. This woman apparently thought that if she could physically lay hold of the tassel, she would mystically contact Jesus' prayer power and be healed. Apparently, clothes did matter. However, it wasn't the garment that healed her; it was her faith.

- **Writing styles:** In our day and age, Paul might send an email, distribute a PDF, or set up a blog for people to read his New Testament letters. His structure, however, is very different from ours. What goes first when we write a letter? Well, the date, then four spaces, and the return address. Then you put "Dear so-and-so," and you're off and running. Then, after all is said, you write, "Sincerely, ME." But when you receive a letter, note, email, or text, what is the first thing you look for? You want to know who sent it. That's right! With a note, you go to the bottom to see whom it is from. Maybe letters should *start*, not end, with the author. And if you look at each of the letters of the New Testament, that is exactly what you will find.

- **History:** Consider issues of history such as political rulers, dates, governmental offices, and other important details. Were you aware that Tiberius Caesar (the ruler when Jesus was alive) was one of the worst of all the Roman emperors and the first to demand worship as a god in his own lifetime?[2] Did you know that Pilate was a racist, especially against the Jews?[3] Herod the Great had two of his own sons strangled.[4] According to tradition, Emperor Nero assassinated Peter and Paul the same year he himself was forced to commit suicide.[5] These facts are not recorded in the Bible, but knowing a bit of history reveals greater depth and sharper contours as you study God's Word.

- **Culture:** This would include social customs, values, and traditions. Did you know that approximately 92 percent of the population lived on the brink of starvation in Jesus' day?[6] Are you aware that Jewish men sometimes wore earrings and Jewish women wore nose rings? Here's another interesting tidbit: Jews were more likely to have a goose as a pet than a dog. Which was the most common method of assassination in the first century: drowning, poisoning, crucifixion, or burning[7]?

- **Environment:** What did Jesus mean when he said, "It will be fair weather, for the sky is red"? Which animal was the most efficient means of transporting goods: camel, horse (with a cart), donkey, or ox (with a cart)[8]?

Check out the answers in the endnotes.

Culture Shock!

We live in a world remarkably different from what is described in the Bible. Consider the culture shock Paul would feel if he rose from that dead and showed up in the United States or another Western nation: (1) He would be shocked at the relationships between men and women. Our open communication and physical touch would border on profane. Female politicians, soldiers, police officers, and teachers would all be outrageous for the apostle. (2) The amount of money we have and how we hoard it would be mind-boggling. Paul would have to wonder why our rampant wealth isn't used even more to extend the kingdom of God. (3) Our individualism would seem odd because he was raised in a communal culture. Our passion for solitude, privacy, personal rights, and individual expression wouldn't just be selfish; it would be seen as unwise, undesirable, and unsafe. (4) Our emphasis on entertainment rather than social development would simply mystify Paul. (5) Our fear of ridicule for our faith? He surely would scorn it as radical infidelity to Jesus, who suffered on our behalf. (6) Paul would probably love our educational systems, technological advances for evangelism, and a government that attempted to serve the poor rather than abuse them as slave labor. (But we do wonder if he would use a Mac or a PC.)

Our lists could be much longer, of course. Yet this much is all the evidence we need to ask some questions about the background of the text. These simple questions will keep you on fertile soil in historical background: Who? What? When? Where? Why? How? Pretend you are a crime-scene investigator! You need to pay attention to things that normal people miss. How? Just be patient, and we will map it out clearly in a moment.

Why should you be concerned about the historical background of a text?

1. **A text cannot mean what it never meant.** In other words, if you apply a passage to a contemporary setting that goes beyond what the author would affirm

to his own audience, then you have not interpreted the text; you have manipulated it. So before we apply the text in the 21st century we must retrieve it from the first century.

2. **Christianity is historically based.** If Muhammad never actually existed, the tenets of Islam would not be invalidated. The same can be said for Confucius, Krishna, and Buddha, and their respective religions. However, if Jesus never existed, Christianity is a misguided superstition that we would do well to abandon.

3. **Knowing history will allow you to read the Bible and know the bigger issues and story that were taking place.** Take a moment and read Psalm 51 armed with the knowledge that Nathan the prophet had just confronted David over his acts of adultery and murder. Or read Philippians 4:4-7 in light of the fact that Paul had been in prison for nearly four years.

4. **Finally, you cannot properly understand the New Testament without understanding the Old Testament.** This is true for EVERY book in the New Testament (well, OK, you *might* get away with reading

Philemon without knowing Moses). The Old Testament is the *assumed* background of the New Testament, and those unfamiliar with it are at an automatic disadvantage. It's kind of like going to an opera or a cricket match. If you don't know the language or the rules, you are confused and inevitably bored. That is not because cricket and opera are boring (millions of people are fans), but because you don't understand them. Our disinterest in the Old Testament says more about our narrow view than its "boring" contents.

How to Access the Historical Background of a Text

Historical background is like mining for gold. You dig through a lot of dirt before finding precious metal. OK, here's what you've been waiting for: three sources for historical investigation.

First, *your best historical source is **the Bible** itself.* It is a big book with lots of stories, and all of them are in a Jewish, Middle Eastern setting. That is our target area, so the Bible becomes your greatest historical source. Let's say you want to study shepherding. Search your computer concordance for *shepherd* and you will land on passages like Psalm 23, Ezekiel 34, Zechariah 11, and John 10 (we'll talk more about concordances in the next chapter). These texts offer insights on the life, work, and heart of shepherds in ancient Palestine.

Second, *augment your reading of the Bible with a **Bible dictionary** or a **Bible encyclopedia.*** Look up your topic (alphabetically) and see what an expert in the field has to say about <u>a</u>griculture, <u>b</u>uilding, <u>c</u>hildren, <u>d</u>ogs...<u>X</u>erxes, <u>y</u>outh, <u>Z</u>edekiah.[9]

Third, *look on a **map*** to help you locate places in the Bible. Don't be satisfied merely with the standard maps you find in the back of your study Bible. You should find maps that show topography, distance, and even weather conditions, such as the satellite images available through Google Earth®.[10] In addition to maps, check out **photographs** that are available online.[11]

Finally, *there are many **websites*** that look at the latest and best discoveries of archaeology and how this science confirms the Bible's historical, cultural, and geographical references.[12]

This history stuff is so cool. Let's have a little fun with the story of David and Goliath in 1 Samuel 17. Take a moment and read the context of that chapter. Then focus on 1 Samuel 17:54. When I read that, I think "gross." That's just nasty. Why in the world would David take Goliath's head to Jerusalem?

Did he want to show his people that couldn't be at the battle? Did he want to celebrate? Was he bragging to his friends? Was it like a hunter with a trophy deer?

Why Jerusalem? What was the author's AIM? Why did he make a point to tell us that David took Goliath's bloody head to Jerusalem? Why did he think we needed to know that? The author hadn't yet mentioned Jerusalem in 1 Samuel. So where was the last time the Bible talked about it?

Answer: Read Judges 1:21 and Judges 19:10-12. Do you see it? Look closely. Why wouldn't David, this Jewish man, spend the night in Jebus (Jerusalem)? It's because the Israelites didn't control Jerusalem yet. It wasn't their city—yet.

You mean to tell me that this teenager took the head of Goliath, the most famous warrior in all the land, to the gates of a city that his people didn't even control? The Israelite army goes one way and David "headed" the opposite direction? Why? What was he thinking? Why would you take a giant's head into enemy territory? What would you be trying to prove?

David knew exactly what he was doing. He already knew he wanted to rule from Jerusalem. He stood there with a giant's bloody head and basically said, "Remember me; I'll be back!" That's awesome!

OK, one last angle here. Turn to 2 Samuel 5. It starts off by telling us that David became king over all of Israel. Now take a look at the section that begins with verse 6. Do you see it? One of the first things that David did when he became king was to conquer Jerusalem. To this day, Jerusalem is called "The City of David." He knew exactly what he was doing with Goliath's head that day! The Jebusites saw him coming, and you can bet they remembered that kid who left a giant's head sitting outside their gates. You just don't forget a teenager like that.

Conclusion

The volume of historical material available online provides even the casual Bible student a look into the culture, politics, geography, and society of the Bible, with greater clarity than ever before. This study of history is amazing. When you read about a city you've never heard of, research and see what happened there before and after the specific passage you're reading. When you stumble on new names, find out who they are, who their relatives are, and just ask why they are even mentioned. You may not always like history class at school, but treat this like you are doing an investigation. It is a ton of fun when you start finding how Bible stories relate.

Going Further

- Just for fun, read 2 Samuel 24:16—two other big things happen at this same spot on Mount Moriah. See if you can figure out what they are, and why God would be "grieved" when the angel got to this location.

- Read the introductions of two commentaries on the biblical book that contains your passage from the assignment at the end of Chapter 2, and answer these questions: Who wrote the book and to whom did he write? When did he write the book? What was the author's relationship with the recipients of the book? What was happening to them at the time the author wrote the book?

- Print out your text and highlight specific items that you think require historical research. If you were transported back in time into your text, what things could you see, feel, smell, taste, or touch? Using a Bible encyclopedia or dictionary, write a brief paragraph describing each item.

CHAPTER 5

WHAT'S THE WORD?

Have you ever heard a preacher say, "The Greek word really means _____"? Sometimes a really good teacher pulls something out of a passage that just blows you away, and you wonder how in the world they figured that out. Buckle up. You are about to learn their secret.

Words are fascinating little things. You live in a culture where words can be short, like when you send text messages. You live in a world where words can be limited, like 140 characters or less on Twitter®. Let's take a look at how this impacts your study of Scripture.

Caution: Words, outside of a sentence, are often meaningless because they can mean too much. For example, take the simple word *hey*. What does that mean? That depends entirely on what follows it: "Hey, jerk" (said by a girl to a guy); "Hey, stop" (said by your mom); "Hey, you" (said by a flirting cheerleader); "Hey, now" (said by a basketball coach with two seconds left in the game). Words without sentences can be worthless.

Understanding the meaning of a word in the Bible will NOT help you understand the author's intended meaning unless you know how it functions in the sentence and on the lips of the one who used it. For example, if you read a phrase like "You won't die," or "Your life will be spared," what does this mean? When we read this kind of phrase in Genesis 3:4, it is a lie told by Satan to Eve about eating the fruit. She and Adam did die. In 2 Samuel 19:23, this kind of phrase was a promise that David would not execute Shimei for previously cursing the king. In these different contexts, the same phrase means very different things.

Dive into these word studies hard. They are fascinating and terribly rewarding. We hope you love this exercise. But never, never, never forget that the purpose is always to understand the author's intended meaning (AIM). With that said, let's get down to business.

First Things First

Words are slippery little things. Before trying to grab hold of them, let us give you several insider tips that will help you.

1. **Words have both denotation and connotation.** Just because you know what the dictionary says about a

word—the denotation—does not mean you know what an author means—the connotation. On any given day a foreign exchange student is likely to hear: "Cool," "Sweet!" "Get out!" "He's hot," "What's up?" or dozens of other sayings. This is just the way we talk. We use words in the hallway and cafeteria in ways you won't find in the dictionary.

2. **English translations do not exactly or consistently represent the Greek and Hebrew word.** Remember, the words we are defining in the Bible are not English. So we need to get back to the original words in Greek and Hebrew, the languages used to write the Bible (we will show you a way to do this later in the book).

3. **Religious terminology.** Some words—such as *righteousness, communion, worship,* and *sin*—have meanings within Christianity that are more specific than their use outside the church. This is not surprising. Certain subcultures use specific words in particular ways. We need to be careful with these words. Before racing to the Christian definition, we should first learn what the word meant in the broader culture and then narrow it down to how the writer used it in a biblical passage. It might surprise

you just how much more meaningful these words can become. For example, *redemption* was a fairly ordinary word in the slave trade. It was the price paid to purchase a slave. *Redeemed* means we were bought with a price that shifted our ownership from one master to another.

How Do You Define a Word?

To determine a word's meaning, *you could look it up in the dictionary*. However, while dictionaries are convenient, they don't always tell the deeper meaning. For example, the dictionary can't quite explain love, mercy, or hate the way those things really feel in everyday life.

Instead of defining a word with the help of a book, consider its meaning on the street. How are people actually using this word? *A word means what the author uses it to mean.* If a word is to be used in a brand-new way, there must be a social group large enough to use its new definition. This sometimes happens through an influential leader or popular figure whose followers use the word enough for it to become well known. Or it could arise from a group working in areas such as medicine, fashion, economics, or sports. As a result, most words have a range of meanings.

Because words can mean several things, *we always must read in* **context** to determine how this particular word is being used in this particular instance.

Time to experiment! Get online and let's do this together. This is going to be fun! Given these tools for determining a word's definition—dictionary, common usage, and context—how does one relate these to biblical words that were originally in Greek and Hebrew? The answer is actually easier than you think.

First up, pick a unique word from your text—the one you've been using in all the assignments so far—that seems to be important or interesting. Follow these instructions below:

1. **Dictionary**—Here is a helpful strategy for looking up your word in Greek or Hebrew.

- Go to blueletterbible.com.

- Type the reference to your text in the search box at the top of the page and hit enter.

- Once the verse comes up, you will see several little buttons to the left with the letters K, C, L, V, and D. Each of these buttons opens up a different tool that you really should explore, but the one of interest now is C. Click on it, and you will see the verse written in either Hebrew (Old Testament) or Greek (New Testament). Find your word, click on the number beside it, and you will see all kinds of helpful information about the Greek/Hebrew word including a dictionary definition AND every use of the word in the Bible! This leads us to step 2.

2. **Common Usage**—Once you find all the times a particular Greek or Hebrew word was used, read them. That's right, *all of them*. That is really the only way to know what a word means—by reading how it was actually used. A concordance is a helpful tool that lists all the times a specific word is used

in Scripture—and the cool thing about a computer concordance is that you easily can look up phrases as well as combinations of words using search criteria such as "AND," "OR," "NOT," or other combinations. Before moving on, play with this just a little bit on blueletterbible.com. It's so cool.

3. **Context**—Read your Bible! We mean it—read your Bible! This is the most neglected practice in Bible study. We listen to all kinds of experts and trust their opinions, rather than reading God's own message and trusting the guidance of the Holy Spirit. Please don't misunderstand: The Holy Spirit can also guide you through teachers, writers, counselors, and scholars, but the place to start and finish is in the Scriptures themselves.

Steps for Researching a Word

Now that you know tools for doing a word study, it is time to walk through an actual word study. These are not to be followed in mechanical precision, but for the first couple of times you research biblical words, following these steps can assure good results.

1. **Context**—Read the sentence and paragraph in which your word is found. Get the general idea of the author's topic, mood, and argument.

2. **Translations**—Look up your passages in about five English versions to see how your word is translated. Again, if you use blueletterbible.com, after you've typed in your reference, you can click the V button and multiple translations appear.

3. **Concordances**—This is the core of your word study! Spend most of your time here reading passages that actually use your word. As you do, try to categorize the uses of the words. Pretend that you have three to five folders (but not more). Each verse must be slipped into one of the folders and labeled with a category that fits all the verses in the file. For example, if we were defining the word *tree* in English, we would find that it is used of a plant, a family genealogy, and an organizational chart. So these would be the three labels on our folders, and each usage we run across needs to fit into one of the folders. As you make

your imaginary files, notice any clusters of words
you find in the concordance. Is your word used a lot
in a particular passage or by a particular author?
All of these may show a unique use of the word at a
particular place and time.

4. **Dictionaries and Word Studies**—Only *after* you have
   looked up every usage of your word and put them
   into categories should you refer to dictionaries and
   word studies performed by scholars. (For dozens
   of examples of word studies by a Greek expert,
   Kenny Boles, professor of New Testament at Ozark
   Christian College, go to markmoore.org/classes/
   principles/wordstudies.shtml.) They will sharpen
   your own thinking. But if you look to them first,
   you will be biased toward their reading rather than
   doing your own thinking. This is not to say that you
   are smarter than experts in the field. However,
   your own discoveries can be more meaningful than
   secondhand sources.

5. **Commentaries**—A commentary explains each verse
   in detail. Any thick commentary will help with major
   word studies. After doing your own research, read
   two or three commentaries on your text and see

what they have to say about your particular word. Thomas Constable, senior professor emeritus at Dallas Theological Seminary, has made all of his commentaries free online as PDFs (soniclight.com/constable/notes.htm).

6. **Context**—When all is said and done, go back to where you started. Read the passage again (and again), and decide which of the folders your word belongs in. The definition of your word should be an exact replacement of the word in context.

Conclusion

Words are the building blocks of language and an indispensable part of any Bible study. The bad news is that word studies are complex and sometimes baffling. The good news is that by following the exercises we've designed, you can research the meaning of Greek and Hebrew words without actually knowing those languages. Through the use of computer concordances, you can do study that a generation ago was limited to the scholarly towers of seminary. Much of this stuff can even be done on a smartphone! Be patient with yourself as you learn this new skill. It takes time and sometimes a bit of coaching, but the end result is a new awareness of the rich fullness of biblical language. That will make all your efforts worth the time and energy invested.

Going Further

- Circle three to five words in your passage for major word studies. There are several key elements to look for when trying to determine which words are important for major word studies. (1) Look for words that seem to be pivotal for the meaning of your passage. (2) Look for words repeated in your text. (3) Look for theologically loaded words. (4) Look for perplexing or unclear words and figures of speech. Sometimes I'll just read a passage out loud and see which word grabs my attention. These guidelines will lead you to the major words to study in more depth.

1. Go to blueletterbible.org. First, save this page as one of your favorites so you can reload it quickly when you need to.

2. Type Acts 2:38 into the search bar and hit enter.

3. Click on the C button to look up the Greek words of this verse.

4. When the page loads, find the word *baptism*. How is it spelled in Greek? Now click on the number "907" to see every use of this word in the New Testament.

5. How is this word defined? How many times is it used? Pay attention to the little box labeled "Search Results" to see which books use it and how many times. Which book uses it the most?

6. Now scroll down and read each use.

7. Scroll back up the page to read the little article "Outline of Biblical Usage."

8. Go back to step two and click on D for the dictionary. Choose *Naves Topical Bible*. Read through the passages listed there.

9. Now write your own paragraph of what this word means and how it is used in the Bible.

10. Go back to step two and explore each of the other buttons to the left of Acts 2:38 just to see what tools are available there. Surf around on this program for at least 15 minutes. Sure, it is easy to get lost. But remember, you are not going to break it, so just play and enjoy.

CHAPTER 6

BIFOCALS AND
BIBLE VERSES

How to Use Parallel Passages

This is actually one of our favorite exercises in Bible study. Finding parallel passages is kind of like a treasure hunt. We are looking for other Scriptures that relate to our passage. Try to find people, places, words, or topics tucked away in other texts. These texts are like diamonds we string together to make a beautiful necklace. One text sparkles well enough; together, they are astounding.

Parallel passages help you compare similar Scriptures that you might not even know about. Comparing a text with other portions of Scripture is one of the best ways in the world to make sure you are not coming out of left field with some crazy theological idea. If you can develop your thought with seven to eight texts, instead of just one verse, then you are probably standing on some pretty solid ground.

While the Bible is a collection of 66 books, it all ultimately comes from one God. That is, the Bible is a unified whole. If God is the architect of the Scriptures, then the best and first commentary on the Bible must be the Bible itself. Taking one verse out of context is really dangerous.

Let's take a look at a simple example. John 15:16 says, *"the Father will give you whatever you ask for, using my name."* Sweet! God, you know I want a Ferrari and an all-expense paid vacation to the Bahamas. Wait—is that really what this verse promises? Well, a few parallel passages might just put some context around this promise. Pay particular attention to the bold print, and determine what the Bible does and does not promise through the following parallel passages: *"You can pray for anything, and **if you have faith**, you will receive it"* *(Matthew 21:22). "You can ask for anything **in my name**, and I will do it, so that the Son can bring glory to the Father" (John 14:13). "But **if you remain in me and my words remain in you**, you may ask for anything you want, and it will be granted!" (John 15:7). And even when you ask, you don't get it because **your motives are all wrong**—you want only what will give you pleasure (James 4:3).*

Other parallel passages could be added, but these four should make it obvious that the promise of John 15:16 is not a blank check for spoiled brats. It is a promise from Jesus that, when we carry out his commission, he will support us in every necessary way to accomplish his will in this world. This is just one example of how parallel passages can constrain the meaning of a text and keep interpreters from going crazy trying to prove their point with one verse.

Think of it this way: When we live in real relationships, there is seldom a closed conversation. There is not *the* talk about the birds and the bees, for example. Rather, most parents bring it up at pivotal points in a child's life. The conversation with a 4-year-old about the importance of keeping his pants on at preschool should differ significantly from a conversation with a 16-year-old going out on his first date. Likewise, parallel passages allow us to trace the conversations that God had with his people through the development of sacred history.

Perhaps the most important parallels are those that *don't* use the same words but still talk about the same ideas. For example, a collection of all the texts that talk about divorce, war, family, Jesus' second coming, or salvation can form the foundation of a well-grounded theology. More difficult subjects can only be dealt with fairly if we hear the whole counsel of God, not just those passages that happen to say what we already believe. Sometimes these topics will have a key word that pops up in two or more texts (see how the word *Christian* is used in Acts

11:26; 26:28; 1 Peter 4:16). More often, however, it is the thoughts rather than the vocabulary that are similar (see Matthew 10:37 and Luke 14:26, along with Luke 16:25 and Revelation 6:11).

How to Find Parallels

There are a number of effective sources for finding parallel passages.

1. **Read the Bible.** No, really, read your Bible! As you do, make lists of verses you run across that speak to topics you are interested in. For example, if you are interested in the ways teenagers and young adults can have an impact for God, just find an empty page in the back of your Bible and write the words "Young Examples." Then, every time you run across a verse about a teenager or young adult doing something for God, just jot down the reference. You will be amazed how quickly your list grows as you go to church and regularly read your Bible on your own.

2. **Use the marginal notes.** A good study Bible will put parallel passages in the margins or in footnotes. If you look at the verses in one of these study Bibles, they have little letters in italics after some of the words. These letters correspond to Scriptures found in the margins of the page. Those letters will match up with another verse that relates to the one you are reading. Professional scholars who know the Bible prepare these really well. While they might omit a few texts that you would include or perhaps include a couple you don't think are relevant, the notes generally are extremely helpful and are a quick way of getting two or three parallel passages for any text.

Sometimes I (Jayson) entertain myself by looking up parallel passages. I just start tracking down these references in my study—especially when I find a name or a city in the Old Testament. I like to see what kind of things happened there in the past. Who was related to that person? What other passages connect to this one? I probably get more great insights for sermons and lessons doing this, than through any other form of study that I use.

3. **Use a topical Bible.** Some Bibles are specifically designed to help you get at parallel passages. The *Thompson Chain-Reference Bible* is the best known. Also, some books collect passages according to topics. *Naves Topical Bible* is a classic standard and is free to use online.[13]

Keep in mind, however, the whole point is to let the Bible comment on the Bible. These other references make good walking sticks to support you; just don't let them become crutches that replace your own legwork.

4. **Use a computer concordance.** We have already talked about the use of a computer concordance as a tool for word studies. It is equally valuable for parallel passages. The real advantage of the computer concordance (aside from speed) is the ability to look up phrases, not just words. Let's say you want to investigate miracles. You could type in "miracle* OR heal*" and you would get every instance of *miracle*, *miracles*, *heal*, *heals*, *healed*, *healing*, *healer*, and similar words—all at the same time. This would give you plenty to read. As you read, take note of other synonyms such as *miraculous*, *awe*, *wonder*, *saved*,

and so on. Add these to your search, and in a matter of minutes, you could collect quite a list of biblical texts on the subject.

Conclusion

Parallel passages are a powerful way of allowing the Bible to be your first and best commentary. Because God is the author of the whole collection, it makes sense to see what God said elsewhere in this continuing conversation. As long as we are aware of what God said first, what God said most often, and what God said most clearly, we can fairly develop a collection of biblical texts on certain topics that provide a well-rounded view of God's truths on important doctrines.

Going Further

- Choose three or four topics or phrases from your passage, and find parallel passages that speak to those issues. Once you have found a dozen or so texts for each topic/phrase, write a simple paragraph describing each subject, using nothing but the information from parallel passages. The idea for this assignment is for you to develop a commentary on your text using nothing but the Bible. Pouring yourself into this task will pay great dividends because you will be able to allow the Bible to interpret the Bible without the initial influence of commentators.

CHAPTER 7

THE ART AND DISCIPLINE OF APPLICATION

"So why do you keep calling me 'Lord, Lord!' when you don't do what I say? I will show you what it's like when someone comes to me, listens to my teaching, and then follows it. It is like a person building a house who digs deep and lays the foundation on solid rock. When the floodwaters rise and break against that house, it stands firm because it is well built. But anyone who hears and doesn't obey is like a person who builds a house without a foundation. When the floods sweep down against that house, it will collapse into a heap of ruins"
(Luke 6:46-49).

Allow us to plagiarize 1 Corinthians 13 for a moment: If I memorize the entire Bible and read Greek and Hebrew but do not apply it to my life, I know nothing. If I understand theology, philosophy, and history but do not live out the words in the text, I prove nothing. If I fathom all mysteries and solve all problem passages but do not love God or other people, I accomplish nothing!

The job of the biblical interpreter is not to become smarter but to faithfully apply the written message of God to the community of his people.

Back in the fourth century, Augustine got it right when he said that the goal of all Bible study was to love God and love one's neighbor. The end of Bible study is not just the head, but also the hands and heart.

Before getting into the actual principles for proper application, there is one warning sign we must observe: **If your application exceeds the AIM of the text, your interpretation ceases to share God's authority.** In other words, if you make a promise that the text does not make, God is not obligated to fulfill that promise; after all, it is your promise, not God's. Or if you teach something that is not in the Bible, your fellow Christians are not obliged to agree with or follow your teaching. Or if you give an opinion that the inspired writers do not share, your hearers don't have to follow your example.

Perhaps an illustration would help. Some preachers promise that we will have great wealth if we will simply ask for it and have enough faith in God (and perhaps make a donation). What does this say about the faithful Christians living with torture and poverty in places around the world? Clearly the doctrine exceeds the biblical message and therefore is inaccurate. If your application exceeds the AIM of the text, it ceases to share God's authority. It may still be a good application in certain contexts and it may even produce good fruit, but it is always shaky ground when we try to say more than the Bible itself says.

Good application doesn't happen overnight. It is a process that takes years. Moreover, don't expect steady and predictable growth. Life isn't like that. Rather, we leap from one plateau to another. You may read your Bible for a month or two and really not make much progress, but then you will have an "aha!" moment that puts some pieces of the puzzle together. These moments don't come as frequently, however, without the long, tedious process of daily and habitually feeding on God's Word.

Here are four practical steps that will speed your growth:

1. **Read the Bible.** We know it sounds too simple to even say, but many people talk about the Bible but never actually read it. God intends for the Bible to be understood by the common person. So read it. Start with Mark or John if you are completely new to this. Other easily understood books include James and Proverbs. Acts and Genesis are also exciting historical

books worth reading after the Gospels (Matthew, Mark, Luke, and John). And Romans is probably the most important book of Christian doctrine. These are good books to start with. It will be extremely important to choose a translation that is easy for you to read and understand, if this is to be a regular spiritual discipline. Caution: There is not one right and inspired translation, so stop looking for it. *The best translation of the Bible is the one you will actually read.*

2. **Memorize important chapters of the Bible.** That's right, we said *chapters*. Start perhaps with the Sermon on the Mount (Matthew 5–7) or Romans 8. Print the passage and tape it up in your shower (laser toner does not run in water, or just place it in a plastic storage bag). This will give you a few minutes every day to work on it. Say a phrase out loud over and over again until you can say it completely, without looking at the text. Then move to the next phrase.

3. **Have a Bible with you at all times.** Read on your lunch break or while waiting in a line. The more you feed, the more you'll grow. If you train for a marathon,

you would constantly keep energy bars nearby. A similar truth applies here with the Bible—devour it!

4. **Serve somebody, somewhere, somehow.** If you only eat and never exercise, you won't attain ideal health. You will learn more from your reading if you are giving of your time and using your spiritual gifts in service to the body of Christ or the world at large. We're not merely saying that serving is the end of Bible study; we're saying that serving is the *means* of understanding the Bible better.

Three Targets of Application

When we apply the Bible, we aim for the *heart*, the *head*, and the *hands*. We don't necessarily target all three simultaneously. But eventually, the Bible must affect each of these areas. Some texts will target just one, others two, while others will scatter a shotgun blast across all three. Here's what to look for.

Heart. Scripture between two leather covers is a rather dead and useless thing. Paul urged the text to be inscribed on the human heart (2 Corinthians 3:3). So how do we transfer the text from the page to our heart? There is both a human side and a divine side to this task.

The human side requires a practice called *meditation*. The book of Psalms opens with these words: *Oh, the joys of those who do not follow the advice of the wicked, or stand around with sinners, or join in with mockers. But they delight in the law of the Lord, meditating on it day and night (Psalm 1:1-2).* This Hebrew word for *meditating* indicates something like mumbling. You know that moment that you find yourself singing a song and you don't even know when or how you got started? It's that concept. You think about that text so much that it is always in the back of your mind. You are saying phrases from it as you walk down the hall. You roll it around in your mind, talk out all sides of it, sometimes even debate with yourself. That, in a nutshell, is meditation.

From the divine side, Scripture is written on your heart through the Holy Spirit. Jeremiah 31:33 says, *"But this is the new covenant I will make with the people of Israel on that day," says the Lord. "I will put my instructions deep within them, and I will write them on their hearts. I will be their God, and they will be my people."* Heart transformation goes beyond your study, cleverness, or intellect. It depends on the Spirit of God doing a work in your heart. It requires your heart to be open to the work of God. This means humility, obedience, and love.

This is not magical hocus-pocus. It is not running around saying, "God's Spirit told me this and that." Rather, it is much like two people who have been in a long-standing relationship: twins, best friends from childhood, or an old married couple. They can finish each other's sentences, communicate volumes with a glance, or pick out just the right gift for Christmas. Why? Because they have come to know the other person. Our goal is to align our hearts with the Spirit of God so we can know what God is thinking before he even tells us. How do we do that? By listening as moments turn into hours, hours into days, days into years, and loving as years turn into decades.

Correct hearing has a lot to do with intimate loving. Do you have a favorite teacher or mentor? Isn't it true that you listen to that person more courteously? If we love God, we learn to listen well, and listening well over a long period of time tends to align our hearts.

Hands. Jesus said, *"Those who accept my commandments and obey them are the ones who love me. And because they love me, my Father will love them. And I will love them and reveal myself to each of them"* *(John 14:21).* We don't correctly interpret the Bible until we do what it says. True understanding involves personal involvement so that you *don't* correctly understand something *until* you practice it. "Book smarts" and "street smarts" must collide before Bible study is of real value. So how do you do it? Well, do it! James 1:22-25 offers some pretty good advice:

> But don't just listen to God's word. You must do what it says. Otherwise, you are only fooling yourselves. For if you listen to the word and don't obey, it is like glancing at your face in a mirror. You see yourself, walk away, and forget what you look like. But if you look carefully into the perfect law that sets you free, and if you do what it says and don't forget what you heard, then God will bless you for doing it.

Head. While it would be a gross error to suggest that being a Christian is about adhering to a set of doctrines, it would also be a gross error to ignore the primary points of our faith. We do believe in the bodily resurrection of

Jesus, salvation by grace through faith, God the creator, the inspiration of Scripture, the virgin birth, predictive prophecy, and a bunch of other truths. As you grow in Bible study, you will become more and more proficient in knowing the Scriptures that support each of these doctrines. Be wary of spiritual arrogance, but never shy away from being doctrinally sound. It is your duty and your destiny.

Conclusion

We often spend the bulk of our time in the first-century world looking at the meaning of words, cultural background, historical setting, and other areas. Proper application, however, is the primary goal of Bible study, so this step cannot be short-circuited. It does not require the kind of robust intellectual study of the previous steps. Rather, it demands meditation, spiritual sensitivity, and attention to our surrounding culture. This will require the wisdom of God-honoring men and women to extract and translate the truths of the Bible so the modern person can apply the counsel of God to their lives. You are that person for a waiting and wondering world—waiting for the God of the universe to speak and wondering if God's words can make sense of a shattered and broken world. The message of the Bible can speak; we must give it voice.

Going Further

- Now, write out the application for your text that would apply to your heart, hands, and head—what you should feel, do, and think based on the teaching of your text. These are more powerful spiritual "crowbars" than Greek and Hebrew, commentaries, sermons, and concordances all combined!

CHAPTER 8

IT'S TIME TO EAT

Your ability to devour the Bible matters. It isn't enough to grab the occasional snack or even meals a couple of times a week at church. You must learn to feed yourself. Follow in the footsteps of Jeremiah, Ezekiel, and John, and devour the Word.

We seem to look everywhere for answers except the one place that God tells us to look: in the Bible. Your pastor doesn't have the words that can sustain life. Your best friend doesn't have the counsel to bring healing. The music on your iPhone® won't light your way or keep you from sin.

How can a young person stay pure? By obeying your word (Psalm 119:9).

I have hidden your word in my heart, that I might not sin against you (Psalm 119:11).

Your word is a lamp to guide my feet and a light for my path (Psalm 119:105).

The Word of God matters. It is not like any other book. This book is inspired and equipped to transform your life. You have to devour it. *But you must remain faithful to the things you have been taught. You know they are true, for you know you can trust those who taught you. You have been taught the holy Scriptures from childhood, and they have given you the wisdom to receive the salvation that comes by trusting in Christ Jesus. All Scripture is inspired by God and is useful to teach us what is true and to make us realize what is wrong in our lives. It corrects us when we are wrong and teaches us to do what is right. God uses it to prepare and equip his people to do every good work (2 Timothy 3:14-17).*

So get ready! And here's the secret we've saved for last: When you devour the Word of God, it will also devour you! *For the word of God is alive and powerful. It is sharper than the sharpest two-edged sword, cutting between soul and spirit, between joint and marrow. It exposes our innermost thoughts and desires. Nothing in all creation is hidden from God. Everything is naked and exposed before his eyes, and he is the one to whom we are accountable (Hebrews 4:12-13).*

So here we go! This isn't goat cheese we are talking about here. This is better than Thanksgiving dinner at grandma's. The table is set. It's time to eat this book.

Going Further

- Read Psalm 119 and write down as many metaphors
  as you can find that are used in connection to God's
  Word (such as light, path, honey).

Endnotes

1. Check out blueletterbible.org or studylight.org. Each of these has links to a vast array of Bible study tools including encyclopedias, dictionaries, lexicons, and other resources.

2. Tacitus, *Life of the Caesars: Tiberius*.

3. Philo, *Legatio ad Gaium* 159-161; Suetonius, *Tiberius* 36.

4. Josephus, *Ant.* 16.11 §392.

5. Eusebius, *Hist. eccl.*, 2.25.8, see also Irenaeus (*Haer.*, 3.1-3.3), Tertullian (*De praescriptione*, 36).

6. Richard Rohrbaugh, "The City in the Second Testament," *Biblical Theology Bulletin 21* (1991) 67-75; Walter Taylor, "Cultural Anthropology as a Tool for Studying the New Testament," *Trinity Seminary Review* 18/1 (1996) 13-27; and James Jeffers, *The Greco-Roman World* (Downers Grove, IL: IVP, 1999), 20.

7. The answer is poisoning—which leads us to ask, "Do you know what plants you could have eaten with John the Baptist out in the wilderness?" Probably not!

8. If you chose donkey, you are correct. The roads were so rough that a cart was very difficult to maneuver and would break with heavy loads.

9. For a fine dictionary, see eastonsbibledictionary.com or bible-history.com/smiths. For an encyclopedia, go to studylight.org/enc/isb or christiananswers.net/dictionary/home.html.

10. Check out earth.google.com.

11. For photos of Israel and the Ancient Near East, see freestockphotos.com.

12. For a couple of the best archaeological sites see biblicalarchaeology.org and biblicalarcheology.net. Disclaimer: Remember, not *everything* you read online is reliable. If you have a question you might want to run it past your pastor.